DELIVERANCE
BY FORCE

IDONG WILSON

DELIVERANCE BY FORCE

2nd Edition

ARPress
ILLUMINATING IDEAS
EMPOWERING VOICES

To order additional copies of this book, contact:

ARPress
45 Dan Road Suite 5
Canton, MA 02021

Hotline: 1(888) 821-0229
Fax: 1(508) 545-758

CONTENTS

DEDICATION

Dedicated to my wonderful grandfather
Late Elder Y.E. Udoh, whose prayers and teachings led me
to the Lord of Deliverance.

And to all the oppressed of this world
whose faith in the Lord of Deliverance remains unshakable
no matter what.

ACKNOWLEDGEMENT

I would like to thank the following people for their assistance in the course of preparing this book. Rev. F. W. Umoren of Qua Iboe Church, Uyo Superintendency, Nigeria, took up from where my grandfather stopped in molding me and bringing me out from the land of perpetual darkness into the land of everlasting daylight. He reviewed the work and made useful suggestions, catechisms and corrections. Aniekan Brown of University of Uyo, read through the manuscript for editorial corrections, they deserve my warm appreciation.

I would like to acknowledge the inspiration given to me by late Elder J. T. Obot, and Sister Eno Tom of Qua Iboe Church, 2 Abak Road, Uyo, Nigeria; the Prayer Band of Qua Iboe Church, Oron, Nigeria; and the Prayer Band of QICSFON, Uniuyo Chapter, Uyo, Nigeria in kindling the flame of what God had embedded in me to actualization. May the Almighty God bless them and reward them more abundantly.

For the sizeable and various contributions, good and friendly environment provided by my mother Ms. Aniema

Eakin, brother Rev. Eleazer Eakin, "the real me" Comfort Eakin (my wonderful wife) and my friends especially Dr. & Dr. (Mrs.) Osarumwense Evbuomwan, and the entire Hope Alive Ministry family of Idong Wilson World Outreach, USA, I say God bless you all.

Finally, to my children, Nnonye, for your seemingly irrelevant questions that sure brought relevance to bear and thus inciting me to dust off the manuscript for this publication; Kemfon, for your special rendition of Psalms 23; Enyekeme and Emediong for your understanding and sacrifice of your valuable playtime with daddy for the sake of this project, Thank you so much.

You guys are the best, and to you I say Shalom!

FOREWORD

It is a privilege to be requested to write a foreword to a work that has taken time, revelation and hard work to produce, moreso when one has had the added advantage of studying the manuscript and sharing the deep knowledge revealed in the pages of *"Deliverance by Force"*.

The Lord, Jesus Christ, showed in His Ministry that Deliverance was and remains a major prong of His mission. He executed this, NOT by "settling", "negotiating with", or "appeasing" evil spirits or demons. The Bible uses the words "rebuke", "commanded", "ordered" and words of the genre to describe his deliverance method. Force and compulsion were the hallmarks thereof. Superiority, authority and power were on display.

A cursory check in the Advanced Learner's Dictionary of Current English shows that:

> *"Rebuke"* means to *"reprove, speak severely to a subordinate for being impudent"; "Command"* means *"order, authority, power to control"* and *"Order"* means *"to give an order"*.

The language of Matthew 8 verse 26, Luke 8 verse 24, Matthew 9 verse 32 (to mention a few) is the language of deliverance - the language of force. Deliverance indeed, is by force.

Are you afflicted, depressed, oppressed, or tormented by the evil one? Your deliverance is sure. This book throws more light on this area of Christian authoritative activity. It is my prayer that in reading it, you shall be lead to the God of deliverance who shall surely propel you into your deliverance by force, and you shall act on its message and thereby expand the Kingdom of Jesus Christ on earth as we occupy till He returns. Idong Wilson's first book is an indication that there is in him a well, and we expect several springs to flow therefrom. Amen.

- Elder Uyouko S. Uyouko

FIRST WORD

A man woke up early one morning with a start due to the dream he had that night about being dead in a ghastly motor accident. Thus, he decided never to go out that day. He took his bath, washed his vehicle and sat back in his parlour (living room) to read newspapers and magazines; but before long, his ceiling fan pulled out of place and killed him right there on his couch.

A sister's traditional marriage was fixed and everything was set in place; the invited guests were all seated while waiting for the arrival of the groom. The band was playing, the groom's parents and family members were present awaiting the arrival of their son. They all waited in vain and the young man did not show up, as such, the marriage ceremony was called off only for them to discover that the young groom had been murdered by hired assassins a few hours to the commencement of the marriage ceremony.

A woman was married for over seven years without an issue, and when all hope was lost she became pregnant. There was real joy for her, but it struck that she had to carry that pregnancy for over twelve months and later gave birth to a spool of polythene.

A sister was taken into marriage and she quickly conceived and everyone was happy for the fruitful marriage, she gave birth to a bouncing baby boy who neither sat nor crawl for three good years after his birth and later died.

A man was promoted at his place of work and he celebrated the promotion with a thanksgiving in the church. Barely two weeks after, a message came from home of the death of his mother-in-law; he rushed home for the funeral only to be informed of the serious ill health of his own mother who later passed on. He had to return to his station to source for loan from friends for the funeral of his own mother. Barely a week after the funeral, his one and only son died of an unknown ailment, and two days later the man was relieved of his job.

Afflictions here and there, all over the world, everywhere the story is the same, the list is inexhaustible.

Everyday in our lives we face one odd or the other. In one way or the other, we are being afflicted by our enemy (the devil). The devil, like a roaring lion is tirelessly roaming about seeking whom to devour. The fact remains that once you take a decision for Christ, a battle line is drawn between you and the devil, and in its ploy, afflictions must follow (1 Thess. 3:3, Rev. 2: 10).

It is for this reason that Jesus Christ came to deliver mankind (John 10: 10). Now, the victory over afflictions is real and sure right where you are. It is only left for you to utilize it, you don't have to lament, plead, bargain, implore or solicit with the devil anymore over your afflictions. The devil knows how to afflict but Jesus Christ our Saviour and King specializes in liberating the afflicted. Now that he is here, all you have to do is to simply accept him into your life, your business, your academics, your marriage and your everything and, his liberation power shall be yours. Jesus Christ is here to give you that your much desired "Deliverance by Force" whether the devil likes it or not.

CHAPTER ONE

WHO IS YOUR GOD?

Paul was a man that did know his God, as such, he was strong wherever he was taken to, and was able to do exploits.

In the thirteenth through sixteenth verses of the nineteenth chapter of Acts of the Apostles lies a rather very important and interesting story of how demons could recognize the lordship of Jesus Christ and all that are his, and of course had to ask the plain men (negative practitioners) "Who are you?"

In other words, the demons were telling the seven sons of Sceva; we know Jesus Christ as the Lord of lords; the man whom we all have to bow to; the man that has authority over everything including us; we are all subject to him. As for Paul, we know him as a servant of the only one true and living God who made the heavens and the earth. His God is the ever reigning king. In fact, authority has been given to this Paul by his God to make us subject to his (Paul's) commands.

In short, since his God is the king of kings, and all authority has been given to him over us, we have no other option than to obey his (Paul's) command. But, as for you, we do not know you nor your god. Now tell us, where do you get your authority to command us from and who is your god? We cannot obey an unknown and inferior authority - then came the great disgrace upon them; they were torn naked.

The scripture tells us in Daniel 11:32 that "...the people that do know their God shall be strong and do exploits". You see, when the sons of Sceva were asked, "who are you?" or, put it straight, "who is your god, and where does your authority come from?" Since they did not know the God they were claiming from (Jesus whom Paul preacheth), they were unable to stand before the demon possessed man and could not do any exploit let alone exploits.

Paul was a man that did know his God, as such, he was strong wherever he was taken to, and was able to do exploits. He was imprisoned, and simply because he knew his God the foundation of the prison shook and every prison door was thrown open and every man's band was loosened - what an exploit! He was bitten by a poisonous snake at Malta, contrary to the expectation of the people, he was not harmed because he knew his God.

Because he knew his God, Paul was able to heal the people of all sorts of sicknesses at Malta (Acts 28 1:10). Even his handkerchiefs and aprons were jam packed with healing anointing (Acts 19:11-12) - great exploits!

When God sent Moses to go and deliver the Israelites out of bondage in Egypt, on arrival Moses and Aaron told Pharaoh "We bring you a message from Jehovah, the God of Israel..." (Exo.5: 1). In other words, since they (Moses and Aaron) were Israelis, they were simply telling Pharaoh that their message was from "our God". The God they knew. That was what gave them strength and boldness to stand before Pharaoh - the knowledge of their God.

To crown it all, they did exploits when at the beginning their rod which became a serpent, swallowed up every other rod-turned-serpent in the land of Egypt - wonderful exploit!

Now, who is your God? It is rather disheartening to notice that to some people, money is their god; to some, their god is their connections; education; social status; wife; husband; and children; and yet to some, their god is their cults; associations; church denomination; and even family ties, etc.

3

> *"Pastor, you and your congregation know Psalm 23 very well, but I know the good shepherd of whom the Psalm is talking about..."*

These people if you watch them, are prominent members in their different places of worship. They are the front pew sitters in the church. They even speak in tongues and are termed "holy ghost filled". They go about with the slogan, "give to Caesar what belongs to Caesar, and give to God what belongs to God" (Matt. 22:21 NLT).

In their narrow understanding, they believe that Jesus simply meant their worshiping in the church when occasion demands, and to go ahead and sacrifice to the speechless, eyeless, lifeless and useless gods when they dim fit to do so.

They forget to note that before Jesus made the statement, he had to show the people an image in which the people quickly identified as Caesar's (Matt. 22 :19-21). The understanding of these people are blinded to the fact that they themselves have been identified as images of God (Gen 1: 26-27), but they willingly surrender these images of God to the devil and its agents, only to excuse themselves with that stupid slogan of theirs - Oh! how foolish man is, no wonder they cannot do exploits.

Your power to do exploits depend to a greater extent on your knowledge of the master of all and His redeeming power.

One Sunday morning in a small church, the preacher in charge demanded that the church should recite Psalm 23 as it was their routine before delivering the message of the day. As you may know, this psalm is a very popular one. It is well known to every church goer, even schools in some societies have adopted it as part of their devotional prayers, hence, in those societies almost everybody (if not all) including the children can even sing the Psalm off hand.

In some places, it has become a household song. On this faithful Sunday morning, everyone recited the Psalm as normal as always, but towards the end, a strange old man walked from the back pew to the platform and grabbed the microphone. He then began reciting the Psalms all over again, but this time around with much emphasis "The Lord Is My Shepherd...".

The whole congregation stood still wondering what was becoming of the old man. But before long, people started weeping (as they fell under the anointing of the Holy Spirit introduced through the old man's recitation). Before the old man could finish reciting the Psalms, two third of the entire congregation were weeping seriously (as yokes were being broken). To this end, the preacher in charge and some of his lieutenants were not happy over the strange happenings, and had to summon the old man to meet with the Church committee immediately after service.

On meeting, the preacher in charge was furious as he accused the old man of introducing a strange spirit into the Church. In his rage, he asked the old man; "why was it that when I asked the people to recite the psalm, they did it peacefully and no one wept but when you came with yours everyone was weeping? Don't you know that I am the man in charge here, and that it is I alone that can order and it be done? Why have you decided to bring confusion into the church with that your weeping spirit...?"

The old man simply looked at the preacher in charge with deep pity in his heart, with a wide grin and tears of love rolling down his gentle cheek, he answered: "Pastor, you and your congregation know Psalm 23 very well, but I know the good shepherd of whom the Psalm is talking about, it was him that I introduced to your congregation - "Oh what a knowledge that brought instant exploit!

The presence of Daniel, a man that knew his
God forced all the lions in the den to embark on a
compulsory fast.

You! Yes you out there, who is your god? Who do you know best in your life? Is it the psalms or the good Shepherd?

Your power to do exploits depends to a grater extent on your knowledge of the master of all and His redeeming power.

When Moses and Aaron where being confronted by Pharaoh, asking them "who is Jehovah" (Exo. 5:2), he was simply asking them "who is your God?". Because they knew their God, exploits (Marvelous exploits), such that were never before experienced were theirs - what a thrill!

Shadrach, Meshach and Abednego were a people that knew their God. Oh how I love these young men for their courage.

You see, when there is this knowledge of the only one true God, one is always strong and courageous.

When these young men were brought before king Nebuchadnezzar, and he told them "I'll give you one more chance . . ." (Dan 3:12). These young men did not do as some of us today would do. Some of us would have said, well God knows why he brought us to this land; he knows we do not have any other alternative, after all, 'when you are in Rome, do as the Romans do'. No! They did not say so but stood their ground.

On the other hand, Shadrach would have told the other two, you see, for us to save our neck, when the musicians play let us bend down and lace our shoes, at least the king and all the people will believe we have bowed down to the statue and will let us go unharmed - 'holy tricks', that would have been the name of the game, better still, it would have been called 'smart ideas'.

No! they didn't do that (Matt. 10:39; 16:25; Mk. 8:35; Lk: 9:24). They simply stood firm for the God they knew can save.

Exploits are not for every Tom, Dick and Harry, but only for the elects that know their God and his wonderful saving power.

Anytime I read the passage, I am almost always driven "crazy" at the reply of a people that knew their God; "O Nebuchadnezzar, we are not worried about what will happen to us. If we are thrown into the flaming furnace, OUR GOD is able to deliver us; and He will deliver us out of your hand, your majesty" (Dan. 3:16-17), and this their God did deliver them for real which made Nebuchadnezzar to call them "servants of the Most High God" (Dan. 3:26) and were even blessed by the King and a decree was made " . . . any person of any nation, language or religion who speaks a word against the God of Shadrach, Meshach and Abednego shall be torn limb from limb and his house knocked into a heap of rubble. For no other God can do what this one does" (Dan. 3:28-29) - what exploit can be more than these!

Or, have you forgotten how this same God delivered Daniel out of the lions den simply because Daniel knew "his God"? (Daniel 6).

If Daniel was like some of us today, he would have said, well, God you know my "hands are tied", I have no other option than to obey the authority, and would have quoted Romans 13:1-2. He would have told God, please for these few days permit me not to come to you for anything, please try and understand. After all, you even understand the heart better, I shall only come to you by heart, you know my life is at stake, or, lets change our meeting time, I shall come to you by midnight when all others are asleep, trust me I'll keep to time. Better still, he would have even shut his windows so that no one would know what was going on in his room. No! He stood his ground for the God he knew.

For you to excel in life and really triumph over situations, you must know your God.

When introduced into the lions den, he was seen as a foreign body. The presence of Daniel, a man that knew his God forced all the lions in the den to embark on a compulsory fast. They embarked on hunger strike for this foreign body; this fearsome being to be removed from amongst them lest they perish

- Oh Hallelujah! Even the king had to embark on a tarry night (for he did not sleep throughout the night) for the sake of Daniel - what an honour for a man that knew his God!

Before Daniel was thrown into the den, king Darius made a statement of faith with authority, Oh how I love the statement; "Thy God whom thou servest continually, he will deliver thee" (Dan 6:16). When that God delivered Daniel, he was brought out of the den unhurt.

I am madly in love with the way the Living Bible puts it; "And not a scratch was found on him because, he believed in his God" (Dan 6:23 TLB).

A command was issued that his accusers be brought along with their families into the den, the scripture has this to say; " . . . and the lions had mastery of them, and brake all their bones in pieces or ever (before) they came at the bottom of the den" (Dan.6:24).

This happened simply because these people did not know the living God, hence, the lions had to brake their fast immediately they and their families were thrown into the den, and since they (the lions) were subjected to a compulsory and prolonged fast, they were extremely hungry and so had mastery of the enemies of God.

This forced king Darius to enact a decree that every kindred shall fear and worship the God of Daniel (Dan 6:25- 27) - what an exploit!

How many times has your God been glorified, honoured and worshiped because of you? - know your God!

Do you want to exploit your education, business, health, marriage, finance or wealth? Then know your God, the only one true God, the Alpha and Omega, the ever reigning king and, all things shall be yours to exploit. Daniel did not say " . . . and shall do EXPLOIT" but "EXPLOITS". This simply means unlimited exploits. It is the wish of God that you do exploits (3John 2), it is left for you to decide for yourself whether to exploit that situation of yours or allow it exploit you.

Take a cue form the action of the Israelis when they were liberated from bondage. Listen, they were liberated because they knew their God (Exo. 2:23-25). I so much admire the way the Living Bible puts verse 25, "Looking down upon them (the Israelis), He (God) knew that the time had come for their rescue".

You see, all the while the Israelis were enjoying the Egyptian fries and did not remember (know) their God, as such, God kept silent and overlooked their situation. But when the burden became too heavy for them to carry; in fact, it became unbearable for them, they remembered and cried to their God. He was moved by their cries at recognizing that they could not help themselves and that no one else than God could save them. He (God) then knew that the time had come for him to rescue them, and he did just that.

11

God cannot and shall not rescue you from that situation if you do not realize your helplessness and recognize his presence, i.e if you do not know him. It is only those that know their God shall do exploits.

Exploits are not for every Tom, Dick and Harry, but only for the elects that know their God and his wonderful saving power. No wonder Apostle Paul had this to say in Philippians 3:10 "That I may know him and the power of his resurrection . . .". It is always wonderful and marvelous an experience to know him (the only one true God).

If you know him, nothing, absolutely nothing can stand on your way to exploits. Oh how I wish we all have an in-depth knowledge of him, we would not remain at the complaint counter anymore, for we shall have all had an edge over all situations.

If you want to have an edge over that depressing situation that has been holding you captive for years now, know your God! When you know him, you shall surely exploit the situations. The Israelis knew their God, they were able to exploit their oppressors (the Egyptians) (Exo. 12:36).

Before you stick out your neck to pursue those exploits, stop and answer the ever throbbing question "Who is your God?", and you shall have gotten the answer to your exploits with ease.

A nursery school's pupil was asked to recite Psalm 23 in the class and he said, "the Lord is my shepherd, that's all I want . . .," all attempt to correct the boy from his own version of the Psalm proved abortive, then the principal of the school decide to ask the little boy for his explanation of this new version of the Psalm, and he had this to answer; "last Friday in this class our uncle (teacher) told us how good a shepherd the Lord Jesus Christ is; how he loves us; how he died for our sins; how he rose from the death; and that he is coming back to take us home to live with him for ever in heaven. And, on Sunday, in our Sunday School session our preacher confirmed these to be true.

Now if the Lord is such a good shepherd, why do you say I should not want him?" this time with tears rolling down his little cheek, he affirmed his stand on his own version, " . . . that's all I want, I want him in my everything".

Beloved, there have to be that hunger in you for the one true God. You must have want for him, which shall translate into a need of him always in your life.

There must be that longing in your life for him, and this shall lead you to a deeper knowledge of him. For you to excel in life and really triumph over situations, you must know your God. This is the only key to attaining deliverance by force.

You just don't have to remain a 'professor' anymore, simply open up for him and be real and true to yourself, and life shall be yours to exploit.

If you believe you are a child of the kingdom, and you are still pressed down by conditions; or even slapped by powers and principalities just stop and think, Who is your God?.

CHAPTER TWO

I HAVE SEEN YOUR AFFLICTIONS

Only take care of the centre (give Jesus Christ that express invitation into your all and all) and the circumference will take care of itself. Always know that you have a role to play in your deliverance. You have to help God (by inviting him into your life), for him to help you.

For four hundred years, the children of Israel were in bondage in Egypt. They were slaves to the Egyptians. Because they knew their God, and cried out unto him day in and day out for their deliverance, that God heard their cry and raised a liberator amongst them at the appointed time (Ex. 3:7-9). This deliverance came simply because their cry to the lord was in earnest and with a sincere believing heart.

I don't know how long it has been since that your problem started. I don't know how far you have struggled to free yourself of the bondage. I don't know how helpless you have been in that situation which you find yourself. But, there is one thing that I know and also want you to know, our God is quite able and willing to deliver you out of that bondage if only you will want Him to, and invite him into your life and that situation (Gen. 18:14; Matt 19:26). God's salvation has never before come a shade late. It always arrives right on time.

Just imagine, four hundred years gone by. Generations upon generations lived and died. One would be bound to believe that there would be no way out anymore for these people. After all, they were not the original immigrant to Egypt, as such, they would not know their way back. A trial of this will simply be like knocking ones head on a brick wall. Even if they would get out of Egypt, where would they migrate to? Who would show them the parcel of land that belonged to their forefathers? And, of course, it was possible that their neighbours shall have annexed their land before now.

You see, the Lord Jesus Christ is such a perfect gentleman that does not force his way into any man's house (life). He does not gate-crash into any man's house. He acts only on invitation (Rev. 3 :20).

For them to remain slaves in Egypt would be far better than going out and becoming strangers even in their own land. At least, to any natural man, this sounds like a reasonable and logical line of argument in favour of their continuous stay in Egypt. Afterall, they had enough food to eat in Egypt. They were used to the "Egyptian fries".

It was better they remained there and enjoy all the fries rather than leave their bondage tight to the fries behind and become complete strangers in the face of the globe as they rightly complained (Exo. 14:11-12; 16:3; 17:1-3) But thanks be to our great God, when it was time, He said "it is enough". Thanks also to a man like Moses who never gave up inspite of all odds, and, at last deliverance was sure for the people of God.

Your situation maybe branded "hopeless". But, I know that Jesus Christ is a specialist in bringing joy to the hopeless. He has done it before to the people of old, he has been doing it to others today, why wouldn't he do it for you?

You only have to recognize the presence of the master of situations (Jesus Christ) and invite him into that situation and he shall take care of it all.

To benefit from his deliverance power, you must play your role well; simply invite him into the situation - that is your role.

Just make Him a partner in your afflictions and he shall lighten the bond for you. Only take care of the centre (give Jesus Christ that express invitation into your all and all) and the circumference will take care of itself. Always know that you have a role to play in your deliverance. You have to help God (by inviting him into your life), for him to help you.

You see, the Lord Jesus Christ is such a perfect gentleman that does not force his way into any man's house (life). He does not gate-crash into any man's house. He acts only on invitation (Rev. 3 :20).

If only you will invite him into your life and everything, he shall surely put everything right for you. He specializes in turning the right side of everything up. Simply surrender to him and his lordship; invite him into every facet of your life and your afflictions shall be a forgone conclusion - that is just your role.

Don't you remember brothers Paul and Silas in the Philippine prison? They acknowledged the presence of the master of all in their afflictions and then invited him to share in their sufferings through their praises to him, Immediately the invitation was sent out, the unusual happened, and they were delivered (Acts 16 23-26).

Also, Peter was a prisoner with maximum security accorded him. The church in their prayers invited the Lord of host into that prison and the unusaual happened when every prison door swung open on their own accord for Peter to walk pass.

What is your prison that Jesus Christ cannot bring you out? That is His field of specialization - giving hope when all hope is lost. But, he shall only do it when invited. He changed water to wine at Cana of Galilee when wine was most needed, only on invitation (John 2: 2-3). Also, for this to happen, the people had a role to play and they played it well (John 2:5-8).

To benefit from his deliverance power, you must play your role well; simply invite him into the situation - that is your role.

What about that woman with the issue of blood? She did not allow her situation to be a hindrance to her. It was even her condition that paved the way for her deliverance. You see, she was stinking; when the people perceived her odour they gave way for her to pass.

Because she was determined to make Jesus Christ her partner in that affliction, she did not stay back out of shame but moved on and invited Jesus Christ into her sufferings through a touch of faith; and straight away she was relieved of her affliction (Mark 5:25-29).

She did not procrastinate nor postpone for another day, but made good use of her only opportunity. Now is your time and today is the day of your salvation, don't wait another minute.

Listen, twelve years was long enough a time for any physician to brand a condition "hopeless" after many diagnosis and treatment without any improvement. The scripture tells us that the woman suffered many things of many physicians but her condition rather grew worse (Mark 5 :26). But, when Jesus Christ, the greatest physician was invited in, as a super- specialist, He turned the hopeless situation of that woman to a hopeful one. He gave hope to that woman in a hopeless situation. May even your afflictions prepare the ground and pave a way for your deliverance in Jesus name - Amen!

Bartimaeus was a well known blind man in the city of Jericho. He had his usual place at the gate of the city. He was a symbol of identification, such that if you were to go to Jericho in those days and found not Bartimaeus at the front gate of the city, you would quickly realize that you had gone the wrong place and not Jericho. From the look of things, it seems he was blind from birth (Mark 10:46-52) - affliction!

He had to find a suitable job for himself - begging. His people had to make a comfortable place for him at the gate of the city where he would have to beg for arms from everyone going in or out of the city.

He was nobody to be reckoned with in the society. They made him understand that he had no share with the people in the city. His function was to remain as an identification mark for visitors to the city of Jericho.

He however accepted that role and even found the job to be a lucrative one. He even did it with pride.

He was such a trustworthy servant to the society, he never for once left his duty post. But one day, it occurred to him that the job was too mean and meager for him, and that he had the right to shares of his society.

Suddenly, he learnt that Jesus Christ was passing by, he made up his mind to invite Jesus Christ into his "lucrative profession" - begging. Even though the people rebuked him calling him names; I can visualize some people saying that he was a lazy blind man who would not want to remain and do his assigned duty. Others thought him to be a stupid outcast of the society seeking cheap popularity, yet others thought him to be an idiotic deviant in the society seeking to disrupt the movement of the master and the peace of the society.

Rather than yield to their instructions and rants, I could see him turn around and ask his rebukers, "can you then help me if I keep quiet?" They answered, "how can we?" He then said to them, "then leave me alone to invite the man who can into my business" and continued in his invitation bid to Jesus Christ, and then came the great shocker to the people - his instant healing (Mark 10:46-52).

Beloved of God, don't ever be satisfied in that condition you find yourself, press harder and invite the master of all - Jesus Christ - into that your situation. If there is a best, please don't ever settle for the good. God means the BEST for you. Don't listen to the comments or rants of the distractors; their job is only to weigh you down and not to help you up. You don't have to share your problems with those rumormongers, they are not going to do you any good. It is only Jesus Christ that can make the difference for you. Just invite him to share in your afflictions and situations, and that shall settle it all for you.

One thing I love my Jesus Christ is, he is ever ready and willing to accept any genuine invitation given him, no matter who is involved, where and what it is about. Once you invite him into your life and everything, and allow him the free hand to Lord over you and your all, he will then tell you, "RELAX my child for I have seen your afflictions!"

CHAPTER THREE

POWER TUSSLE

Miracle and magic are two parallel lines which cannot and shall not meet. If for any reason they meet, the difference is always very clear, for miracle must surely override magic.

Whenever two authorities meet, there is always a struggle for supremacy; it is this supremacy that brings about recognition, power and authority. In a bid to gaining this recognition, one authority must try as much as possible to prove its superiority over the other in order to exercise authority over it.

This is exactly what happened when the king of kings through Moses his servant met with king Pharaoh. Pharaoh tried to trick the people to believe that he (Pharaoh) was the most powerful king that can exert authority over everything at anytime. Little did he know that there existed (and still exists) a supreme king that has authority, dominion and power over every situation, beings, spiritual or terrestrial, kings and kingdoms. When Pharaoh tried a bit of his magical art, the supreme king (God) only laughed at him and showed the people His miracle power.

Beloved it is better to have a miracle in your life than receive bunches of magic. Miracle and magic are two parallel lines which cannot and shall not meet. If for any reason they meet, the difference is always very clear, for miracle must surely override magic.

See what happened when Pharaoh's magic met with Aaron's (God's ambassador) miracle, "so Moses and Aaron went in to see Pharaoh, and performed the MIRACLE as Jehovah had instructed them . . . and they were able to do the same thing with their magical arts (this time not a miracle) . . . But Aaron's serpent (miracle) swallowed their serpents (magic) (Exo. 7:10-12). It is worthy of note that, miracle must swallow up magic, no matter their number— what a power!

When king Jesus with His mighty power went into the grave and met with the powers of hades, there was a serious tussle which led to a great earthquake, and an angel was sent from heaven to roll away the stone from the tomb, thereby leaving the guards who were agents of the lesser power lying as dead as logs of wood (Matt. 28:4).

How about when He (Jesus) was on the Cross, when He gave up His spirit to the Father, the power of the master of all subdued the power of the priests and that of the law so much so that the rule that was laid down from ages was broken, here the veil of the temple was divided into two (Matt. 27:51), making it possible for everyone to now be able to boldly approach the throne of grace (the holy of holiest) without fear.

It did not stop there, because of this great power, even the grave could not hold back the saints that were long dead as they were seen testifying of the lordship of Jesus Christ to the people in the city. Not only that, even the laws of nature had respect for this great authority, and a great darkness covered the whole earth for good three hours instead of broad-daylight, from 12 noon to 3.00p.m. (Matt. 27:45; Mk. 15:33; Lk. 23:44) - that's a super power!

When Paul and Silas were imprisoned, they were moving with this super power, that was why the prison yard experienced a great earthquake and the doors could not remain shut anymore neither could the bands hold any prisoner captive anymore for the super power had prevailed in the tussle.

Life is full of tussle. Every authority, force and dominion seeks to gain supremacy over the other. They all try day in and day out to get you under their control. It is you that can decide who to surrender yourself to.

You are a free moral agent, you have the freedom to chose who to serve and be subject to. Whoever you cast your vote for and surrender to is the one to control you.

You are a free moral agent, you have the freedom to, chose who to serve and be subject to. Whoever you cast your vote for and surrender to is the one to control you. You are to make the right choice now. Do it not merely in a haste, use your brain wisely.

Chose the Lordship of Jesus Christ now and He shall lead and control you aright.

Whenever choices are to be made, priority must surely come to play, hence, scale of preference is of utmost importance. What is your preference in life? To be the head or the tail; a freeman or bondman; a son or slave; a victor or vanquish; a success or failure; a governor of subject . . . ?

The choice is yours to make now.

Sometimes ago, situations demanded for the children of Israel to make a choice Moses through the unction of the Holy spirit knowing the folly of man, that man (the Israelis) will rather choose death, quickly admonished them to choose life for their betterment - Deut. 30:19. The same situation has arisen, a choice is here for you and I to make. A warning is being sent to us this day that we choose the Lordship of Jesus Christ that it may be well with us. Remember, "There is no salvation . . ." (Acts 4:12).

I am not trying to say that when you chose Jesus Christ, you shall be entirely free from tussles. No! To think this way would be just like a boxer that goes into his career with the mindset that since he has been trained by an ex-world champion, he shall always walk out of every fight victorious without being hit by his oponents, only to be disappointed with feelings of defeat at the first blow by his opponent in the ring.

Every true Champion goes into a fight with the mindset that though he shall be hit by his opponents, he shall surely come out winning the match. Tussles shall surely come your way but because you have chosen the lordship of Jesus Christ, you are solely for Him, you dwell in Him and He in you, you are now carrying a super power. Yes, a greater authority. Because of this, every other authority shall be under your control. Thus, in every tussle, you shall always be at the head and not the tail (a victor not a vanquish) . . . Due 28 :13.

One day I had a discussion with a brother. Incidentally, I was the man at the complaint counter. I was complaining that though I have seen the great hands of God in my life right from childhood and His miracles to my life, He (God) almost always allows (wants) me to weep before He meets my pressing needs. He always allows great tussles to come my way . . . and I do not like these.

Tussles are for God's glory; utilize it whenever it comes your way for a greater recognition of your God and you.

Back home that night, the Holy Spirit took me on a great expedition where we (the Holy Spirit and I) explored the indepth truth of God's word. At the end of the expedition, I realised why Brother Paul at all times was told "My grace is sufficient for you" II Cor. 12:9, and I could not help, but end up thanking God instead of complaining the more. It dawned on me that I am the one who sometimes delay in making God my partner in whatever I go through. I am the one who always delays His miraculous; He is always ready to act for us.

Maybe you have had experiences that may seem to suggest that God does not care anymore about you - that is a gross mistake for He cares now more than ever. He is only preparing you now to be able to withstand the evil days. Remember the lesson of the eagle. The most important thing here is for you to make the right choice - choose Jesus Christ now - and in the face of every tussle you shall always stand firm as Mount Zion. (Psalm 16:8; 21:7; 46:5; 55:22; 62:2, 6 and 66 :9).

Again, begin now to feed your faith to growth, and starve your doubt to death, then you shall have God at the centre of your life to make you excel in the face of every tussle.

Do you remember how Moses, Joshua, Elijah, Elisha, Daniel, Shadrach and co, Paul and a host of others excelled in the face of their tussles? It is because they made the right choice - the one and only true God. Now, it is left for you to make your own choice. As for me and my household, we are casting our votes for the Lordship of Jesus Christ and only Him alone.

Always be ready for exploits. Fear not when tussles come your way for they are not allowed by your father in heaven for to destroy you but to prepare and equip you for survival in the battle field (the world) exactly the military training does to a military personnel; rather, always be prepared for the divine manifestation of God's supremacy and recognition as well as your promotion in the end.

Tussles are always good for every life at the end. Whenever there is a tussle, there is bound to be a recognition for supremacy and promotion or demotion at the end of it all. When Elijah triumphed over the prophets of baal, God the father was recognised as the only true God by all.

How about when the lions went on hunger strike because of the presence of Daniel, a man that carried the presence of the supreme authority - a decree was made in recognition of the supremacy of God. (Dan 6:25-27). Have you forgotten about that of Shadrach and co? (Dan. 3:28-29). The revised standard version reads thus in verse 30 "then the king PROMOTED Shadrach . . . in the province of Babylon" - Promotion at last.

Tussles are for God's glory, utilize it whenever it comes your way for a greater recognition of your God and you.

Make the right choice now. Chose the lordship of Jesus Christ for He is the way, the truth and the life (John 14:6). With Him, you are sure of victory all the way. Always be ready for exploits, fear not when tussles come your way, but be prepared for the divine manifestation of God's supremacy and recognition as well as your promotion in the end.

Don't die at the complaint counter. Remember, there were, there are, and there shall always be tussles (Power tussles). Subscribe to the king of kings, and fight from the point of victory won for you 2000 years ago on the cross of Calvary - Hurrah! you are the head and NOT the tail.

CHAPTER FOUR

TIME UP!

Yes, there is a right time for everything. For 399 years, the children of Israel were in perpetual suffering; they were brutalized, maltreated, cheated and exploited by their oppressors - the Egyptians. Since it was not yet the right time, God did not do anything to liberate them from that bondage.

"There is a right time for everything" (Eccl. 3:1)

When Solomon was granted the opportunity to put forward his desire in the form of a request, he did not waste time requesting riches, fame, power and the likes, he rather made wisdom his preference. He knew that riches, wealth, fame and power could only come through wisdom. He decided to seek the blesser and not the blessing, thus, he became wealthier, powerful and more famous than he could have thought of - the right choice!

It was this choice of his that led him to understand the indepth mysteries of the kingdom of God. He came to know that, no matter the tussles in life, there is a time for victory and recognition.

Yes, there is a right time for everything. For 399 years, the children of Israel were in perpetual suffering, they were brutalized, maltreated, cheated and exploited by their oppressors - the Egyptians. Since it was not yet the right time, God did not do anything to liberate them from that bondage.

God's timing is always the best. It is always the right time for everything (Gen. 21: 1-2). Though it may tarry, yet it is for the good of the man.

But just at the nick of time, at the dot of the 400th year which was the right time as prophesied long ago (Gen.15:13), God moved in and one of the greatest miracles ever recorded in the history of mankind occurred - their liberation (Exodus) from Egypt. They spoiled the people that spoiled them before, they came out of their bondage with great wealth (Exo. 12:35-36).

God's timing is always the best. It is always the right time for everything (Gen. 21: 1-2). Though it may tarry, yet it is for the good of the man. God allowed Goliath, the Philistine giant and his fellow Philistines to hold sway the Israeli army for a while (1st Sam. 17).

Actually, when the Israelis heard the Philistine's challenge, they were so frightened. To them, the challenge, seemed to have taken a decade, yet God was timing and waiting for the right time to arrive.

When they least expected, and all hopes of withstanding the Philistines was gone, God at His right time brought out David, a very young boy that was not counted for anything by man in the land of Israel except that he was on Saul's staff on a part-time basis, to come and disgrace Goliath and indeed the entire Philistine's army to a great defeat.

And thus, out of nothing (for David was counted for nothing), God defeated the Philistines and gave Israel victory at last - that was the right time. If God had allowed the

Israelis to conquer the Philistines before now, the defeat would not have had much impact in the annals of history. It would have been viewed as one of those normal and usual Israeli defeat of her enemies - No! God had to hold His peace until the right time to make public show of the enemies of His People.

God sent Daniel to Babylon in order for His kingdom will, power and message to be made known to the Babylonians. Daniel interpreted dreams and divine writings and was promoted to the third in command in the kingdom, yet it was not time right enough for God to unveil His plans. But when the right time came, He used the same Daniel to demonstrate His power.v

Now, why didn't God use Daniel when he (Daniel) was in power to preach His (God's) message to the people and sign the worship of the one true God into law in the land?

No! if God had done that, the Babylonians wouldn't have worshiped Him willingly but forcefully, because being the third in command, and most loved by the king, the king would have signed whatever he (Daniel) wanted into law thereby forcing the people to worship the God of heaven not with their whole heart but because the king has said so.

Again, the king would have signed the worship of the one true God into law so as to please Daniel simply because he loved Daniel and feared him, and not because he loved and feared God, and wanted to please God. So, God had to wait for the right time, which created the right impact that made the will of God alone to prevail. And a decree was signed willfully.

The Israelis tried before long to get out of Egypt on their own, all to no avail. But when the right time came, they were being pleaded to go (Exo. 12:31-32) - that was God's time!

Jesus Christ came as a sacrificial lamb to be sacrificed for the sins of mankind. It was destined by the Father for Him (Jesus Christ) to die this way. He himself knew the manner of death that awaited Him. Before now, on so many occasions, the people sought a way of killing Him (John 8:59;10:39) all to no avail, because it was not the right time to sacrifice Him. Just at the right time, God allowed Jesus to be taken away for the fulfillment of His purpose here on earth (Luke 22:53).

What is that thing that has troubled you for sometimes now; that thing which places you at the complaint counter; which makes you gnash your teeth; which changes your facial appearance and complexion? I am not interested in how long it had been there, what I know is that, when the right time (God's time) comes, they all shall be history. You have to wait for the right time. What is worth doing, is worth doing well - they say. Do not over-rush your miracles; simply wait for God's right time to come.

The Israelis tried before long to get out of Egypt on their own, all to no avail. But when the right time came, they were being pleaded to go (Exo. 12:31-32) - that was God's time!

Whenever it is the right time (God's time), everything must inevitably work. Your deliverance must come by force. Whether the devil, your family, the world, likes it or not, it must sure come. No power, force, principality, or dominion can resist God's timing. Never!

No power, force, principality, or dominion can resist God's timing. Never!

When the right time comes, you will only hear the master's voice saying "time up", and all the grips of the evil one on you shall be loosened. It was at the right time that Sarah conceived even though it did not add up or agree with medical scientific standpoint. A time when doctors would say that she had clocked menopause. A time that she was branded barren, when all hopes of her childbearing ability was lost; a time when everyone thought that it was a total impossibility for Sarah to suckle a baby.

But thank God, "menopause" or whatever that may mean, is not founded in the Holy Scriptures, it is purely man-made, and so, it did not and cannot thwart God's plan. Sarah became a mother at the age of 90 years - the right time, for it was God's time.

You do not have to remain at that complaint counter anymore. There is absolutely no prayer that God does not answer. It is only because we do not listen so as to hear the answer when it comes, as such, we become sad thinking that God does not care as to answer us. Thus, in this our ignorance, the evil one capitalizes on it to scoff at us and make us sad the more.

Oh! if we had listened, we would not be living in tears anymore, our names would not be 'LAMENTATION' anymore for we would have heard God saying: "Have it my Son" Or "wait my son (it is not yet the right time for you to have it)" or "no, I won't give it to you for it will not be benefiting to you" for these are the three basic ways God answer prayers.

Learn now to listen, and you shall be glad you did. I know though, there are times that the prince of Persia (the devil) may stand to hinder your answered prayers (Dan. 10: 12-13), but all you need do here is simply "know your God" and He shall sure send help from heaven to fight and deliever your needed answered prayers (Dan. 10:13).

Remember, "the people that do know their God shall be strong and do exploits". One of your exploits is your breakthrough in life as every force shall loose its grip on you, for surely the right time has come and God is issueing the command "Time up!".

CHAPTER FIVE

"LET MY PEOPLE GO!"

---

*Because the children of Israel invited Him (God)
into their afflictions, He simply told them "I have
seen your afflictions" and went on to command
Pharaoh, the source of their afflictions "Let my
people go!"*

Just at the nick of time, the master planner who sees and knows everything gave a command which marked the beginning of an end - liberty for the Israelis in Egyptian bondage.

However, we have to realise here that God did not force His way into these people's problem. Though He saw it all, God was only waiting anxiously to be invited in. And it was only when He was invited into their afflictions that He (God) showed them(Israelis) His supreme action through His command to Pharaoh - "Let my people go!".

Yes, there is no controversy about the omnipotence, omnipresence and omniscience of God. One fact remains true inspite of these, He does not and cannot act on your behalf except you mandate Him to do so. You have to recognize His presence and accept His lordship position, and then invite Him into your situations before He can act for you.

Take a look at the case of Bartimaeus, eventhough God in His omniscience knew that this man was blind and needed healing, He still had to ask the blind man "What do you want me to do for you?" (Mk. 10 :51). He did not force His way into the blind Bartimaeus' situation; He only waited for invitation from Bartimaeus for Him (God) to show case His supremacy over Barimaeus' situations.

Yes! Pharaoh died immediately the command was given, all that remained of him was mere shadow. He was simply awaiting his burial by installment and Moses knew this, that is why he did not bother himself talking about Pharaoh (a dead man) when the Israelis were lamenting that they were all going to perish.

Because the children of Israel invited Him (God) into their afflictions, He simply told them "I have seen your afflictions" and went on to command Pharaoh, the source of their afflictions "Let my people go!".

It is pertinent to state here that, never a time has God ever given this command and any power or situation disobeyed. Moreso, any situation given this command must die out of the victims life, because, this command is not given except when God is annoyed. Who has ever or shall ever be able to withstand God's anger? (Rev. 6 :17). Absolutely nobody!

Pharaoh died immediately God gave that command "Let my people go!" because God was speaking in His fierce anger after seeing the afflictions of His people.

All you need do is, simply invite the Lord of Lords into your situations, into your afflictions let Him be part of that torment of yours and He will bid you to relax for He has seen your afflictions, and in His sore displeasure will command that situation (from the root cause) "Let my people go!".

There is no how He will give this command and that situation would fail to lose its grip on you, and never shall it come to you again. They shall sure become things of the past.

You shall only be remembering them by sheer chance and begin to wonder where on earth they might have gone to and you shall find them no more (Isa. 41:10-12).

Yes! Pharaoh died immediately the command was given, all that remained of him was mere shadow. He was simply awaiting his burial by installment and Moses knew this, that is why he did not bother himself talking about Pharaoh (a dead man) when the Israelis were lamenting that they were all going to perish. Rather than mention Pharaoh, Moses was concerned with the other Egyptians, "don't be afraid ... you shall see them no more" (Exo. 14:13).

I am deeply in love with verse 14 of that chapter (the way the Living Bible puts it), "The Lord will fight for you, and you won't need to lift a finger". When you invite the king of kings into your boat, your boat can never sink. You would not need to lift even a finger when tribulations come your way, for He shall be there to fight for you - Oh what a truth!

Meanwhile, there is a disheartening discovery that a greater number of people do not always allow God to fight their battle for them. When God begins the fight, they will move in and tell God "relax! Let me lift at least a finger so that it may not look as though I did not do anything. I am a man, let me exhibit my prowess". And God will gently leave them alone. But before long, they fail and begin to blame God for leaving them - oh what an idiosyncratic nature of man!

After some days of rigorous training including starving, the eaglet now becomes strong enough and well able to withstand any form of storm that may come its way.

God gives help only to the helpless. You know as well as I do that no one will ever waste his time to help someone who is well able to get himself out of trouble. If I were to carry a bag of cement into a vehicle, and you discover that I can carry the cement without stress, you won't bother yourself with helping me out; but if you realized that I would not be able to do it myself, you would then offer your help - that is the plain truth! This is exactly how God operates with us.

If you need God to command out that depressive situation of yours, simply acknowledge your helplessness and cry out to the Lord as did the Israelis, and He shall surely act for you.

Whenever I read the story of the exodus of the Israelites from Egypt, my heart remains overwhelmed with awe to see God's ability to ever remember and keep His promises from generations to generations. He had promised Abram "Your descendants will be oppressed as slaves in a foreign land for 400 years, but I will punish the nation that enslaves them ... After four generations, they will return here to this land" (Gen. 15:13-16).

After 430 years God failed to forget His promises, but brought to bear His promises, and therefore remains a true and faithful God - He is much more than wonderful.

I don't know the nature of that your problem, I don't know how long it has been there, but I know it is not up to 400 years. And I know one thing, He has promised long ago to deliver you from that problem.

Learn the lesson of the eagle. A story has it that whenever the eagle wants to lay it's eggs (the eagle usually lays between 1 to 3 eggs per egg season), it will search for the highest spot available in that vicinity, it maybe a tree top, a mountain top or even on the ground if there are no other options available. There, the eagle will make a wonderful and beautiful nest, lay it's egg, and keep guard of the place to ward off any would be predator from getting near the egg.

After hatching, it takes real good care of the young eaglets, and even feeds it with milk and flesh from other birds and animals. The eagle spends time and make a even more comfortable nest for its young one with feathers from other birds.

After a few weeks, the eagle changes its attitude, the once caring and loving mother eagle now becomes wild and awful. It tears the once beautiful and comfortable nest apart and throw out the now frightened eaglet.

When you are depressed, cry out to God; when you are down, cry out to Him; when there seem to be no way out for you, cry out to Him; cry, cry, cry out unto God for He alone can make the difference for you.

Here, the eagle is very much aware of the fact that if the eaglet should hit the ground from that high point, it shall surely die, so it times the fall very well such that it swoops and carry the young eaglet up when it is about to hit the ground and releases it again. This action is repeated again and again. By so doing, the young eaglet learns to fly by flapping its wings though with fright.

When it might have attained that fit of flying, the mother eagle will now watch out for a stormy day and carry the young eaglet to where there is no trees or mountains for the eaglet to perch and allows it to be tossed there up and down, to and fro by the tempest.

It is said that in all these, unknown to the young eaglet, the mother eagle does not leave the young one alone, but is always keeping watch and protecting the young one from afar.

After some days of rigorous training including starving, the eaglet now becomes strong enough and well able to withstand any form of storm that may come its way. The story teller now concludes that this is what makes the eagle the strongest bird on earth; it can fly from Nigeria to Canada without perching anywhere and without being tired.

However, from the story the fact remains that at first, the eaglet always thinks that the mother is heartless, ruthless and was in hatred with it, not knowing that on the contrary, the mother eagle is much caring for it, mindful of it, loving it with its tender heart of a mother, and was only equipping it to be able to withstand the evil days.

This is exactly what God does to His people. He sometimes allow His people to be tempted, but moves in on time and deliver them out from it all (Ps. 34 :19). He does these to equip you against the evil days. All you need do is, just like the frightened eaglet, recognise that you cannot help yourself, and in that your helplessness, cry out to the Lord (Ps. 34 :17- 18) and He shall surely act on your request.

Cry out to Him. The children of Israel did and their cry yielded a positive result from God who commanded their problem from its source, "Let my People Go!". When you are depressed, cry out to God; when you are down, cry out to Him; when there seem to be no way out for you, cry out to

Him; cry, cry, cry out unto God for He alone can make the difference for you. He has promised to answer everyone that cries out to Him (Ps. 50 :15;91:15; Jer. 33:3; Rm. 10 :13). He has never for once lied before, and cannot lie now, He is not ready to experiment on it now.

Oh! how He kept His promises to the Israelites. After 430 solid years of a promise, He still remembered to do excatly that which He promised at the appointed time - Oh! how I love Him for that - He has never for once gone back on His promises - what a retentive memory!

Not even the most complex and excellent computers in the world can do this far. What a promise (covenant) keeping God! Always true to His words (Deu 7 :9; Ps. 146 :6; Eze.

12:28; Mk. 13:31; Luke 21:33).

On the whole, if you want God to command that depressing situation in your life to let go of you, you have to help God in order for God to help you. All you need do is, recognize your helplessness and cry out to Him saying "God please help my helplessness" and then surrender your all unto Him - that is how you can help Him.

Let Him own you, body, spirit and soul. Let Him Lord over your all, and He shall surely put a smile on your face as you claim (by faith) His deliverance power. And you shall only hear His gentle voice commanding that situation out "Let my People Go!"

CHAPTER SIX

MIDNIGHT OF DELIVERANCE

However, in all cases midnight usually ushers in the dawn of a new day; a day of new beginning where things can never remain the same again.

To every person there is a midnight. Midnight may differ from person to person, but definitely it must come in a lifetime.

Midnight is that time in life when every hope of survival is nowhere to be placed. A time when you look to the right, left, front, back and center for help, all to no avail. It is a time when you are completely pushed to the wall by circumstances; and you shout at the top of your lungs, yet there is no one to help you out.

It is a time when all your friends and loved ones are nowhere to be found. At midnight, it always seems as though the end of everything has come; as though the whole world is collapsing in on you. All the forces at work at this moment are always up against you and you envisage no means of survival.

The truth is, where there is no midnight, there can be no dawn of a new day. In view of this, we need not cry for the midnights not to come, but we should be praying for the grace to stand and not to perish in our midnights.

Naturally, it is at midnight that sicknesses increase their hold and torment one the most. Mr. Death is much powerful, and he captures life most at this time. Thieves and robbers normally come calling at midnight, because they know that this is a time of little or no help.

However, in all cases midnight usually ushers in the dawn of a new day; a day of new beginning where things can never remain the same again. So, when you come to your midnight, stand firm for that is the eve of your miracle; and the dawn of a new day (new beginning), for no midnight has ever or can ever remain forever.

The children of Israel were in their midnight when their workload was increased due to Moses' attempt to liberate them *(Exo. 5:4-18)*. They were in their midnight when the Egyptian army almost rounded them off by the Red Sea *(Exo. 14:5-12)*, but because Moses knew his God and also led the Israelis to Him (God), they were able to do exploits. It then dawned on them the day of new beginning - a day of everlasting joy *(Exo. 15)*.

I don't know what your midnight is and how fierce it is, but I know that even as much as the midnight specializes in rolling tears out of your eyes, Jesus Christ specializes in rolling you into a new man - a man of hope, peace and joy with a future - immediately after that midnight. It is rather very unfortunate that Moses died when the promised land was at hand.

No doubt, nobody tends to ever like midnights, but God always allows it to come our way for our own good. The truth is, where there is no midnight, there can be no dawn of a new day. In view of this, we need not cry for the midnights not to come, but we should be praying for the grace to stand and not to perish in our midnights. The important thing here is for us to be able to stand through our midnights, for there is great joy at dawn. It would be so disastrous for one to give up at the eleventh hour *(midnight)*.

Disheartening it is indeed that greater a number of people give up their faith and hope in God when their dawn - the dawn of their new beginning; dawn of their joy; when God is about to turn the right side of everything in their lives up for them; the answer to their many years of prayers; the end of their captivity is at their door step (at hand).

I don't know what your midnight is and how fierce it is, but I know that even as much as the midnight specializes in rolling tears out of your eyes, Jesus Christ specializes in rolling you into a new man - a man of hope, peace and joy with a future - immediately after that midnight.

Understand this, when the good things of life are taken away from you, God is preparing a way for the best to come in. Joseph was deprived of the hospitality of his father's home; he was dumped in the cold outside there in a pit, he was sold out into slavery, he was later given a home in the dungeon as a prisoner - all these constituted his midnight.

Inspite of all these, Joseph stood his ground for the only one true God who specializes in putting smiles on the faces of every man that waits upon Him. Soon the dawn arrived, and then that same Joseph was made a king - at dawn. Promotion always awaits those that put their total trust in God.

Oh, How I love this our God! He knows how to change situations. Always and always, there is promotion immediately after every midnight.

See, no midnight has ever or shall ever remain forever, so be strong and identify with the lordship of Jesus Christ and it shall soon be over, for your promotion is come (Rev. 2:10).

Take a look at Shadrach, Meshach and Abednego, they were taken into captivity in the land of Babylon; in a way, they were prisoners of war. Their names were changed from the original (Daniel 1: 6 &7); they were thrown into a fierce burning furnace - all these were their midnights. After all these (their midnights), they were promoted (Daniel 3:16- 30), because they did not dash their hope nor trade away their faith in the God of heavens.

When the children of Israel were in their midnights, they were totally exploited, spoiled and castigated. But when the midnight was over and there came the dawn, they in turn spoilt their spoilers (Exo. 12:36) - God of wonders! Captors now became themselves captives, Hallelujah!

Our God is so real. I implore you to wait upon Him and He shall bring your dawn to fruition with celebrations of promotion.

God shall sure spoil your spoilers, oppress your oppressors and put in captivity your captors for you. He shall give you power to overtake your enemies after your midnight - at your dawn(1Samuel 30:8, 18-19).

See, no midnight has ever or shall ever remain forever, so be strong and identify with the lordship of Jesus Christ and it shall soon be over, for your promotion is come (Rev. 2:10).

When you feel that you can help yourself and begin to fiddle with it without Christ, God will simply hands off His help. But when you acknowledge your helplessness and yield totally to the lordship of Jesus Christ, He shall then sure come into your midnight and bring you out into a glorious dawn, for He alone holds the key to daybreak.

Do not look for help anywhere else, for God always sends help to His people at midnight (Exo. 12:29-31; Acts. 16:25-26).

You may say: "mine is too tough". Yes, may be your midnight (problems) is insurmontable and has many facets. You have tried so many things, all to no avail, no remedy has yet come. You may have tried so many gods and they have all failed you; they cannot help you out, as such, you have since resigned your plight to fate.

I want you to know that God did not destine you for sufferings. His plans (thoughts) for you everyday are those of good and not of evil (Jer. 29:11); it is His wish that you should be in good health and prosperity (3 John 2).

Oh! if only you would know this and come all out for Him, He is well able to put everything right for you, do not lose hope, make Him your hope.

> *You must not die in your midnight when there is the master of dawn right before you waiting to be invited into your midnight for a turn around.*

If anybody had cause to brand his/her situation hopeless, it is that woman with the issue of blood. She was in her midnight (sickness) for good twelve years - a time long enough for lost of hope. She had tried everything possible (but Jesus Christ), yet to no avail. She had spent everything she had in search of healing, and the Bible says the situation was worse everyday.

Nevertheless, one thing stands out of this wonderful woman, upon all she went through, she did not lose her hope of healing. Despite her disappointments, she kept on trying until she tried Jesus Christ, the one who has never for once failed anybody that comes to Him and that trial paid off and made the difference for her.

Bartimaeus is another person that had every right and reason to have resigned his condition to fate. Afterall, he was blind from birth; "God wanted it so", at least common sense would make man to think, reason and believe so.

Besides, before now there was no history or record of any blind man from birth gaining sight anywhere in the world, so for Bartimaeus to gain His sight was viewed as a total impossibility. Therefore, he took up a suitable and lucrative job - begging. Equally, a wonderful office and home was made for him to carry out his trade at the entrance gate of the city. He ought to have been satisfied with these (as many people would) and settle down for his business believing that he was destined to be blind and a begger for life - this was his midnight.

All along, he never thought of leaving his duty post nor trying out anything or anybody for help, he was contented that God wanted him to be in that position. But one day, his eyes of understanding were opened.

Bartimaeus came to himself realizing that God wishes him to be in good health (3 John 2), and that blindness is not a sign of good health, and thus, not God's wish for him, then he decided to do something different by trying the never changing God, and the difference was clear as the trial paid

The unbelievable was made manifest, thus, the face of history was forever altered - what a challenge meeting God!

Your case is not different. If all others have failed you, why not try my Jesus Christ? He is unfailing.

You must not die in your midnight when there is the master of dawn right before you waiting to be invited into your midnight for a turn around. If there is a best, do not settle for the good.

Don't quit now for quitters cannot win. Plan now to win, endorse the lordship of Jesus Christ and you shall come out smiling and rejoicing at dawn.

The darkest part of the night
Is always the nearest to morning God is faithful to
give the assurance Everything's gonna be good
Refrain:
It's gonna be good (2 times) In the morning
Move on weary pilgrim For everything's gonna be
good

Remember, people don't plan to fail but they fail to plan, so act now.

Maybe you have been living in one problem after the other and you have been trying so many things and ways out, yet to no avail. Please don't resign your condition to fate since Bartimaeus did not, but found the answer at dawn.

The woman with the issue of blood, even though she had spent everything she had gaining no healing, did not quit but pressed on and went home at last rejoicing.

You too can change your situation by pressing on to the never changing God. You can be the next to testify with joy.

Other problems (midnight) in times past had weighed you down and prevailed on you, this very one shall never succeed if and only if you shall rise up and invite the Lord Jesus Christ into that your midnight and surrender to His Lordship.

Then, hold your peace and see the salvation of the Lord as He rolls you into the dawn of your breakthrough with joy and gladness for this is your midnight of deliverance.

This book "DELIVERANCE BY FORCE" I believe is born out of the inner burden of the writer. I am also sure there has been much prayers coupled with fasting prior to the writing of this book.

During my proof reading, I was touched by the inspiration of the writing. Those who read it will derive immense blessings, and not only that, others will be recommended to the Lord of DELIVERANCE through this book.

It is my prayers that many of our young boys and girls will be given the talent and inspiration of writing useful books like this one for Christendom. SHALOM!

- Rev. F. W. Umoren (JP